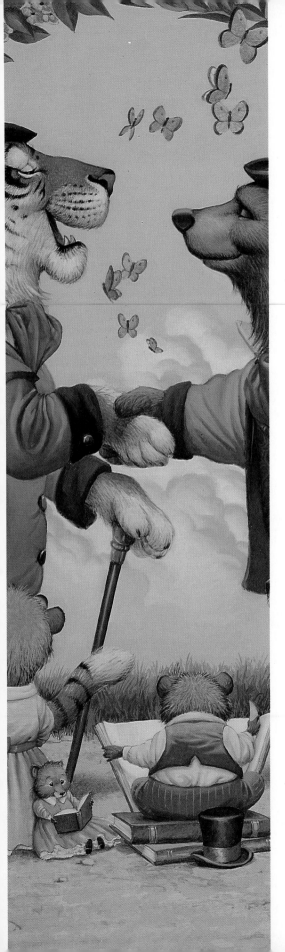

HBJ TREASURY OF LITERATURE

LET'S SHAKE ON IT!

SENIOR AUTHORS
ROGER C. FARR
DOROTHY S. STRICKLAND

AUTHORS
RICHARD F. ABRAHAMSON
ELLEN BOOTH CHURCH
BARBARA BOWEN COULTER
MARGARET A. GALLEGO
JUDITH L. IRVIN
KAREN KUTIPER
JUNKO YOKOTA LEWIS
DONNA M. OGLE
TIMOTHY SHANAHAN
PATRICIA SMITH

SENIOR CONSULTANTS
BERNICE E. CULLINAN
W. DORSEY HAMMOND
ASA G. HILLIARD III

CONSULTANTS
ALONZO A. CRIM
ROLANDO R. HINOJOSA-SMITH
LEE BENNETT HOPKINS
ROBERT J. STERNBERG

HARCOURT BRACE & COMPANY

Orlando   Atlanta   Austin   Boston   San Francisco   Chicago   Dallas   New York
Toronto   London

Printed in the United States of America

ISBN 0-15-301360-5

3 4 5 6 7 8 9 10   048   96   95   94   93

Acknowledgments

For permission to reprint copyrighted material, grateful acknowledgment is made to the following sources:

Clarion Books, a Houghton Mifflin Company imprint: Five Little Monkeys Jumping on the Bed by Eileen Christelow. Copyright © 1989 by Eileen Christelow.

Ell-Bern Publishing Company (ASCAP): "You'll Sing a Song and I'll Sing a Song," lyrics and music by Ella Jenkins. Lyrics and music copyright © 1966, assigned 1968 to Ella Jenkins.

Harcourt Brace Jovanovich, Inc.: Cover illustration from The Cow That Went OINK by Bernard Most. Copyright © 1990 by Bernard Most.

HarperCollins Publishers: Cover illustration from And I Mean It, Stanley by Crosby Bonsall. Copyright © 1974 by Crosby Bonsall. Who Will Be My Friends? by Syd Hoff. Copyright © 1960 by Syd Hoff. "Very Tall Mouse and Very Short Mouse" from Mouse Tales by Arnold Lobel. Copyright © 1972 by Arnold Lobel. From Some Things Go Together by Charlotte Zolotow. Text copyright © 1969 by Charlotte Zolotow.

Little, Brown and Company: Cover illustration by Giles Laroche from Sing a Song of People by Lois Lenski. Illustration copyright © 1987 by Giles Laroche.

Lothrop, Lee & Shepard Books, a division of William Morrow & Company, Inc.: How Joe the Bear and Sam the Mouse Got Together by Beatrice Schenk de Regniers, illustrated by Bernice Myers. Text copyright © 1965 by Beatrice Schenk de Regniers; illustrations copyright © 1990 by Bernice Myers.

Orchard Books, New York: Together by George Ella Lyon, illustrated by Vera Rosenberry. Text copyright © 1989 by George Ella Lyon; illustrations copyright © 1989 by Vera Rosenberry.

Philomel Books: Whose Baby? by Masayuki Yabuuchi. Copyright © 1981 by Masayuki Yabuuchi.

Random House, Inc.: Cover illustration by Lynn Munsinger from My New Boy by Joan Phillips. Illustration copyright © 1986 by Lynn Munsinger.

Marian Reiner, on behalf of Lilian Moore: "Friend" from Little Raccoon and Poems from the Woods by Lilian Moore. Text copyright © 1975 by Lilian Moore.

Western Publishing Company, Inc.: Cover illustration from Me Too! by Mercer Mayer. Copyright © 1983 by Mercer Mayer.

Handwriting models in this program have been used with permission of the publisher, Zaner-Bloser, Inc., Columbus, OH.

Photograph Credits

6–7 (all), HBJ Photo; 10–11, HBJ Photo; 38, HBJ Photo; 63, SuperStock; 64, HBJ Photo; 90–91, HBJ/Maria Paraskevas; 92, HBJ/Rich Franco.

Selection Art

Vera Rosenberry, 10–35; Jackie Snider, 36–37; Eileen Christelow, 38–62; Masayuki Yabuuchi, 64–89; Syd Hoff, 92–107; Bernice Myers, 108–136; Diane Borowski, 137; Arnold Lobel, 138–144

Illustration Credits

Table of Contents Art
Nathan Jarvis, lower right, 5; Roseanne Litzinger, lower left, 4; Gerald McDermott, upper right, 4, center, 4,5

Bookshelf Art
Gerald McDermott, 6,7

Unit Opening Patterns
Tracy Sabin

Theme Opening Art
Sue Williams, 8, 9

Dear Reader,

A good way to meet new people and go to new places is right in your hands. The pages of this book will let you meet many new characters and will take you to new places. You'll read about two friends that dream the same dream. You'll see that a bear and a mouse can find something they both like. You'll see that people can be different but also alike.

Story characters can be your friends. You might find that you and they laugh at the same things or cry at the same things. There are many people and animals to meet. Turn the page and say hello.

Sincerely,
The Authors

LET'S·SHAKE·ON·IT!

CONTENTS

FRIENDS LIKE US / 90

THE COW THAT WENT OINK
BY BERNARD MOST

All the animals laughed when the cow went OINK. This made the cow sad. Then the cow met a pig who went MOO. This story tells what happened when the cow and the pig got together. AWARD-WINNING AUTHOR

MY NEW BOY
BY JOAN PHILLIPS

A little black puppy finds a boy of his own. The puppy teaches the boy all kinds of games and tricks. You will laugh at the funny things in this story. AWARD-WINNING AUTHOR

HBJ LIBRARY BOOKS

OINK OINK

AND I MEAN IT, STANLEY
BY CROSBY BONSALL

"And I mean it, Stanley!" A young girl is making something special. She doesn't want Stanley to see it. What is the girl making? Who is Stanley?

CHILDREN'S CHOICE

SING A SONG OF PEOPLE
BY LOIS LENSKI

Follow a boy and his dog as they walk through a busy city. You will meet many kinds of people along the way.

AWARD-WINNING AUTHOR

ME TOO!
BY MERCER MAYER

A boy's little sister always wants to do everything he does. When he goes fishing, she says, "Me too!" Then she catches the biggest fish. What does little sister do when she has a candy cane and her brother says, "Me too"?

AWARD-WINNING AUTHOR

LET'S GET TOGETHER

Who are the people that are special to you? Read about some friends and families.

TOGETHER

by George Ella Lyon
pictures by Vera Rosenberry

You cut the timber
and I'll build the house.

You bring the cheese
and I'll fetch the mouse.

You salt the ice
and I'll crank the cream.

Let's put our heads together

and dream the same dream.

I'll drive the truck
    if you'll fight the fire.

I'll plunk the keys
if you'll be the choir.

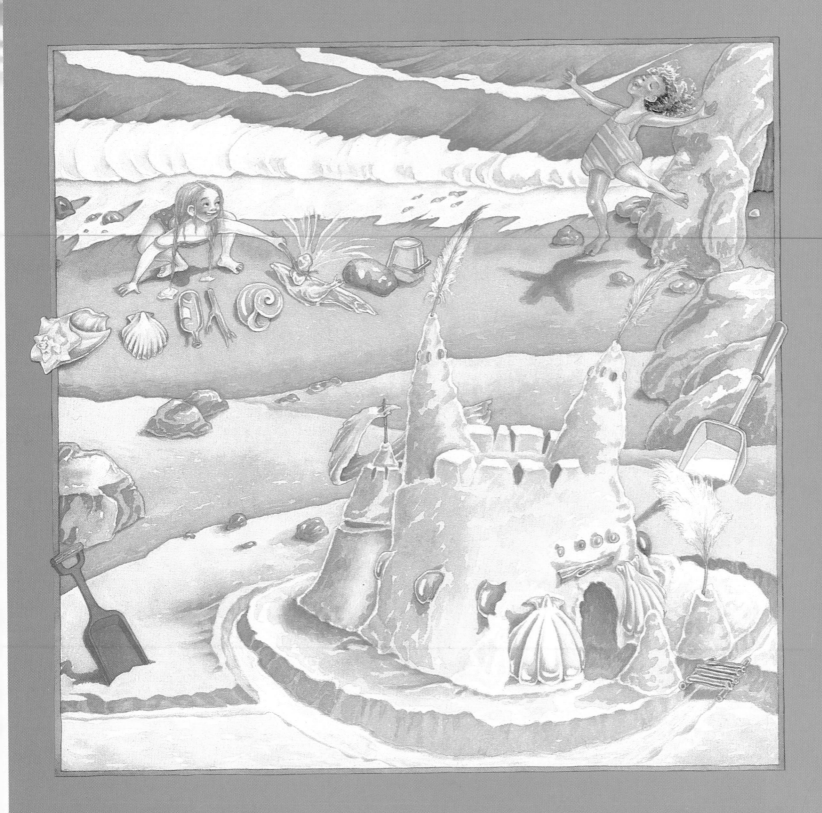

I'll find the ball
if you'll call the team.

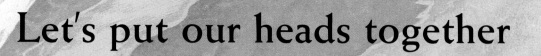

Let's put our heads together

and dream the same dream.

You dig for water
and I'll make a pail.

I'll paint the boat
   if you'll set the sail.

You catch the fish
and I'll catch the stream!

Let's put our heads together

and dream the same dream.

words and music by Ella Jenkins

illustrated by Jackie Snider

PARENTS'
CHOICE

You'll sing a song and I'll sing a song,
Then we'll sing a song together.
You'll sing a song and I'll sing a song
In warm or wintry weather.

You'll play a tune and I'll play a tune,
Then we'll play a tune together.
You'll play a tune and I'll play a tune
In warm or wintry weather.

Five Little Monkeys Jumping on the Bed

EILEEN CHRISTELOW

CHILDREN'S CHOICE

It was bedtime. So five little monkeys took a bath.

Five little monkeys put on their pajamas.

Five little monkeys brushed their teeth.

Five little monkeys said good night to their mama.

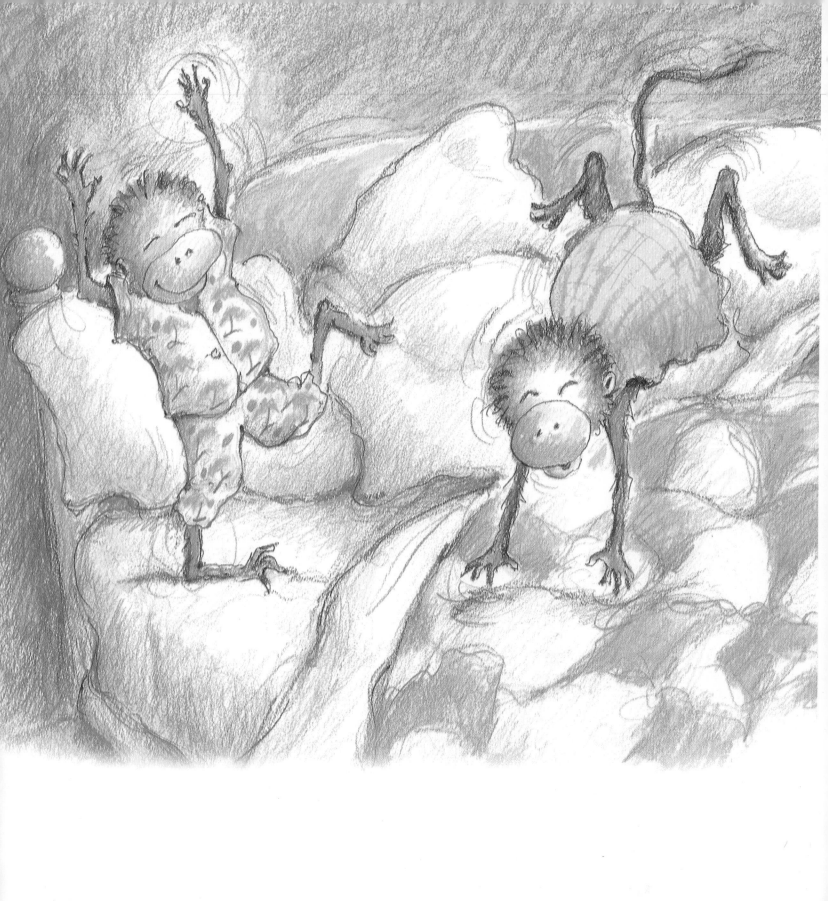

Then . . . five little monkeys jumped on the bed!

One fell off and bumped his head.

The mama called the doctor. The doctor said,

44

"No more monkeys jumping on the bed!"

So four little monkeys . . .

45

. . . jumped on the bed.

One fell off and bumped his head.

The mama called the doctor.

The doctor said,

"No more monkeys jumping on the bed!"

So three little monkeys jumped on the bed.

One fell off and bumped her head.

The mama called the doctor.

The doctor said,

"No more monkeys jumping on the bed!"

So two little monkeys jumped on the bed.

One fell off and bumped his head.

The mama called the doctor.

The doctor said,

"No more monkeys jumping on the bed!"

So one little monkey jumped on the bed.

She fell off and bumped her head.

The mama called the doctor.

The doctor said,

"NO MORE MONKEYS JUMPING ON THE BED!"

59

So five little monkeys fell fast asleep.

"Thank goodness!" said the mama.

"Now I can go to bed!"

Some Things Go Together

**FROM
SOME THINGS GO TOGETHER**

Peace with dove
Home with love
Gardens with flowers
Clocks with hours
Moths with screen
Grass with green
Leaves with tree
and you with me.

by Charlotte Zolotow

Garden in Bloom
Claude Monet
1840–1926

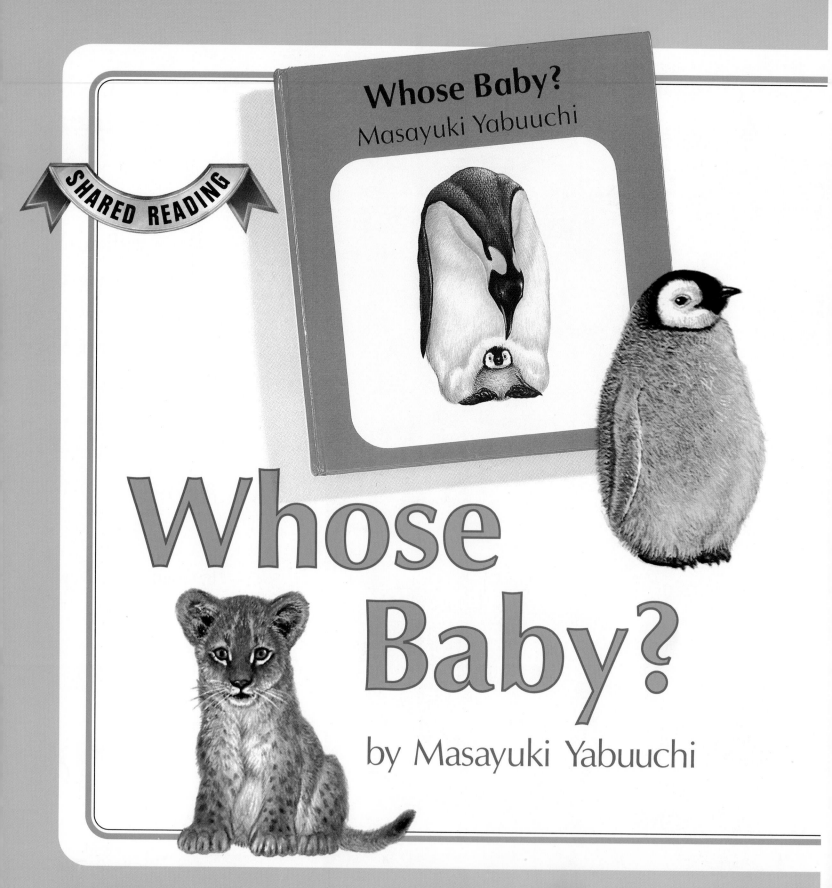

Whose Baby?
Masayuki Yabuuchi

Whose Baby?

by Masayuki Yabuuchi

This is a fawn.
Whose baby is it?

A fawn is a baby deer.

It belongs to a mother
and father deer,
called a buck and a doe.

It belongs to a peacock
and peahen.

73

This cub is curled up fast asleep.
Whose baby is it?

It is a fox cub.

It belongs to a fox and a vixen.

This cub is wide awake —
whose cub is it?

It belongs to a lion and lioness.

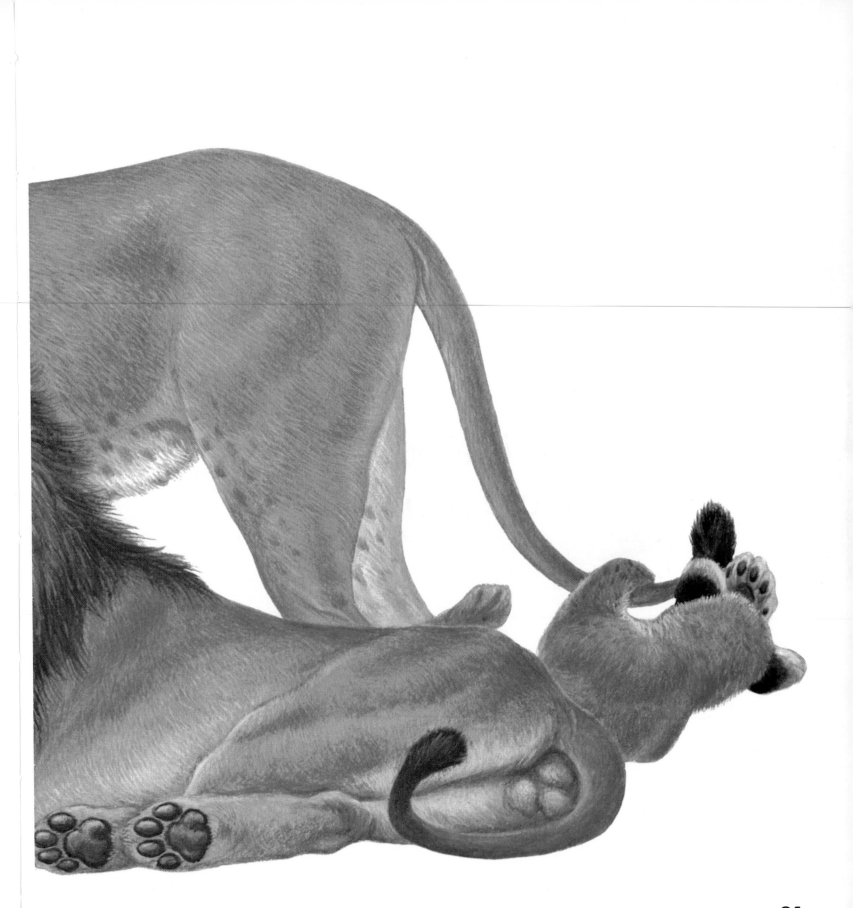

It belongs to a bull seal
and a cow seal.

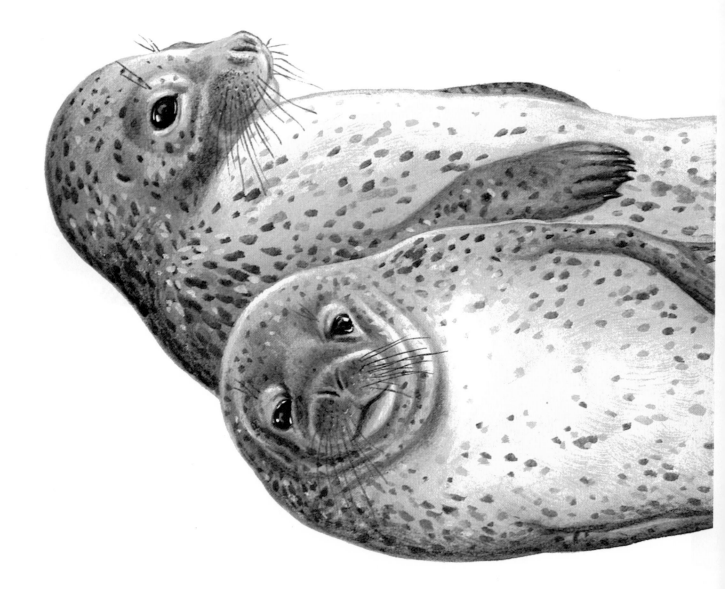

This is a calf.
Whose baby is it?

It is a baby bison.
It belongs to a bull bison
and a cow bison.

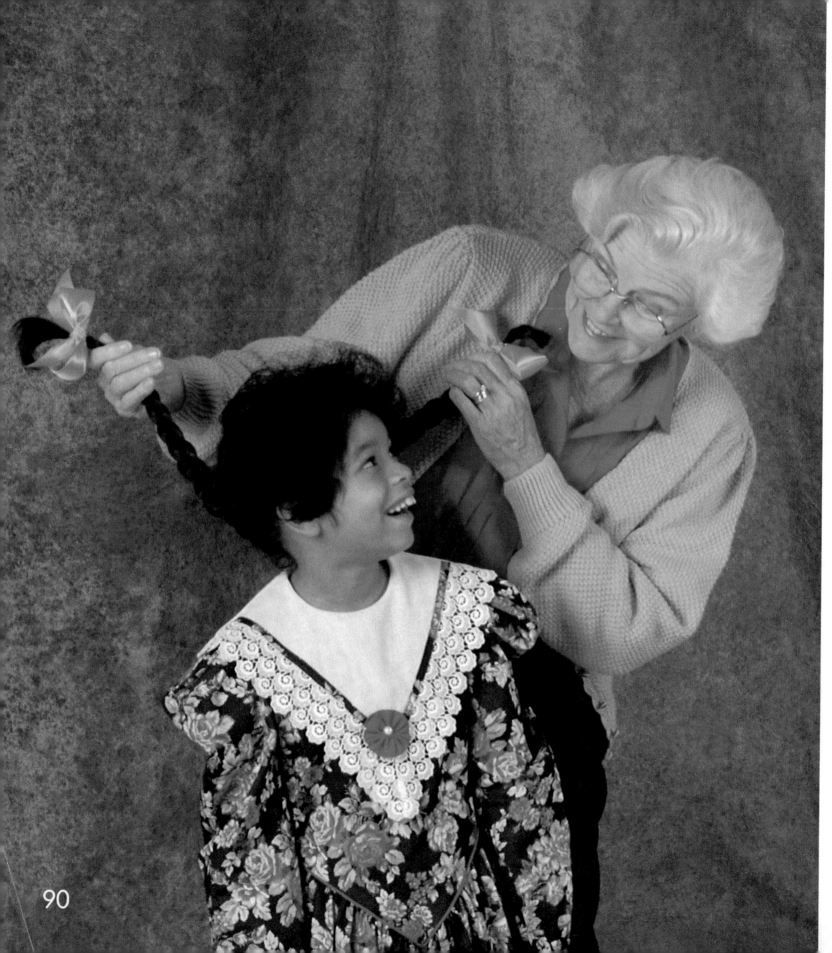

FRIENDS LIKE US

What does it take to be a friend?
Here are some stories about how
friendships work.

CONTENTS

Who Will Be My Friends?

story and pictures by

SYD HOFF

Freddy moved into a new house.

He liked his room.

He liked the street.

"Who will be my
friends?" he asked.

He rolled his ball
to a little dog.

He rolled his ball
to a cat.

They did not roll it back.

"Who will be my friends?" he asked.

"I am your friend,"
said the policeman.

"I am your friend,"
said the mailman.

"I am your friend,"
said the street cleaner.

"Let's play ball,"
said Freddy.

"I have to walk my beat,"
said the policeman.

"I have to bring the
mail," said the mailman.

"I have to clean the street," said the street cleaner.

"Who will be my friends?" asked Freddy.

He went to the playground.

Boys were playing ball.

"Who will be my friends?"
asked Freddy.

The boys went right
on playing.

102

"I guess I will have to
play by myself,"
said Freddy.

He threw his ball
up in the air—

—and caught it.

He threw his ball up

in the air—

—and caught it!

He threw it still higher—

—and caught it!

"Who will be my friends?"
asked Freddy.

"We will," said the boys.
"We need someone who can
throw and catch like that."

"Let's shake on it,"
said Freddy.
And they did.

HOW JOE THE BEAR AND SAM THE MOUSE GOT TOGETHER

BEATRICE SCHENK DE REGNIERS

ILLUSTRATED BY
BERNICE MYERS

Call me Joe.

Call me Sam.

110

Hi, Sam.   Hi, Joe.

Where are you going, Sam?

Where are YOU going, Joe?

112

I am looking
for a place to live.

I am looking
for a place to live, too.
We can live together!

113

I like to live
in a BIG house.

I like to live
in a little house.

Then we cannot
live together.
Boo hoo.

Boo hoo.

Do you like
to play ball?

Yes.
I love to play
ball.

We can play ball together!
I like to play football.

I like to
play baseball.

Then we cannot play ball together. Boo hoo!

Boo hoo!

Do you like music?

Yes.
I love music.

Do you like
to ride a bike?

Yes.
I love to ride a bike.

We can ride a bike together!
I like to ride slow.

I like to ride fast.

Then we cannot
ride a bike together.

Boo hoo.

Boo hoo.

We can play music together!
I like violin music.

I like drum music.

I hate violin music.

Then we cannot
play music
together.

Boo hoo.
Good-bye, Sam.

Boo hoo.
Good-bye,
Joe.

Where are you going,
Sam?

Where are YOU going,
Joe?

It is three o'clock.
I am going to get ice cream.
Every day at three o'clock
I eat ice cream.

I am going to get ice cream, too.
Every day at three o'clock
I eat ice cream.

What kind
of ice cream
do you eat,
Sam?

130

All kinds of ice cream.

131

I eat all kinds of ice cream, too.

Then we can eat ice cream together!

You will live in a big house.
I will live in a little house.

You will play football and ride slow.
I will play baseball and ride fast.

You will play violin music.
I will play drum music.

But every day
at three o'clock . . .

Yes. Every day
at three o'clock . . .

135

FRIEND

When
he wills
his quills
to stand on
end

I'm very glad
that
I'm a friend

of
Porcupine.

by Lilian Moore
illustrated by Diane Borowski

VERY TALL MOUSE AND VERY SHORT MOUSE

FROM *MOUSE TALES*

BY ARNOLD LOBEL

Once there was a very tall mouse

and a very short mouse

who were good friends.

When they met

Very Tall Mouse would say,

"Hello, Very Short Mouse."

And Very Short Mouse would say,

"Hello, Very Tall Mouse."

138

The two friends would often

take walks together.

As they walked along

Very Tall Mouse would say,

"Hello birds."

And Very Short Mouse would say,

"Hello bugs."

When they passed

by a garden

Very Tall Mouse would say,

"Hello flowers."

And Very Short Mouse

would say,

"Hello roots."

When they passed by a house

Very Tall Mouse would say,

"Hello roof."

And Very Short Mouse

would say,

"Hello cellar."

One day the two mice

were caught in a storm.

Very Tall Mouse said,

"Hello raindrops."

And Very Short Mouse said,

"Hello puddles."

They ran indoors to get dry.

"Hello ceiling,"

said Very Tall Mouse.

"Hello floor,"

said Very Short Mouse.

Soon the storm was over.

The two friends

ran to the window.

Very Tall Mouse held

Very Short Mouse up to see.

"Hello rainbow!"

they both said together.